Create Your Own Balcony Garden

A Guide for Beginners

ELVIRA RICCI

TABLE OF CONTENT

Introduction

Balcony gardening is a great way to bring nature into your home, while also having a little bit of fun. It's easy to get started and, with a little bit of effort and creativity, you can quickly create a beautiful and lush oasis on your balcony. Whether you're looking to add a few colorful potted plants or create a full-fledged vegetable garden, balcony gardening offers a great way to get your green thumb going without taking up too much space.

The key to successful balcony gardening is planning. Before you start to purchase plants and supplies, take the time to sit down and plan out your space and decide what you would like to grow. You’ll want to consider the size of your balcony, the amount of sunlight it receives, and the type of soil or containers you’ll need. Consider what types of plants you’d like to grow and pick something that will do well in the space. If you’re new to gardening, start off with something easy like herbs, succulents, or flowers.

What Is Balcony Gardening?

Balcony gardening is a type of urban gardening that involves growing plants on a balcony. Balcony gardening is a great way to bring nature into an urban environment and to take advantage of the space available on a balcony. It is also a great way to grow plants in a limited space.

Balcony gardening has become increasingly popular in recent years. This is due to the fact that more and more people are living in apartments and are looking for ways to have a garden in their living space. Balcony gardening is a great way to do this.

When it comes to balcony gardening, there are a number of things to consider. The first is the size of the balcony and the amount of space that is available for gardening. Balconies come in a variety of sizes, so it is important to consider how much space is available for plants.

The next thing to consider is the type of plants that you want to grow. There are a variety of plants that can be grown on a balcony. These include vegetables, herbs, flowers, and even fruits. It is important to consider the types of plants that will thrive in the amount of sunlight available on the balcony.

It is also important to consider what type of soil is available on the balcony.

This can vary depending on the location of the balcony and the type of plants that are being grown. In general, a mixture of compost and soil is recommended.

Finally, it is important to consider the type of containers that will be used for balcony gardening. Containers can range from traditional clay pots to plastic containers. It is important to select containers that will be able to support the plants and will provide adequate drainage.

Balcony gardening is a great way to bring nature into an urban environment. It is a great way to take advantage of the limited space available on a balcony and to grow plants in a limited space. By considering the size of the balcony, the type of plants that you want to grow, the type of soil available, and the type of containers that will be used, you will be able to create a successful balcony garden.

Choosing the Right Soil

Balcony gardening for beginners can be a great way to enjoy the outdoors and grow plants and vegetables in a confined area. However, in order to be successful and have a thriving balcony garden, it is important to choose the right soil. Here are some important things to consider when selecting the soil for your balcony garden.

1. Structure: The structure of the soil is an important factor to consider when selecting the right soil for your balcony garden. Soils come in various consistencies, ranging from sandy to clay, and each type of soil has its own unique benefits and drawbacks. Sandy soils are easy to work with, but they don't retain moisture very well. Clay soils, on the other hand, hold moisture better, but it can be difficult to work with because it is heavy and dense. It is important to choose a soil that is well-structured, so that it can provide adequate moisture and nutrient retention for your plants.

2. Nutrient Content: The nutrient content of the soil is another important factor to consider when choosing the right soil for your balcony garden. Nutrient-rich soils contain essential nutrients that are important for healthy plant growth, such as nitrogen, phosphorus, and potassium. A soil test can help you determine the nutrient content of the soil and can help you choose the right soil for your balcony garden.

3. pH Level: The pH level of the soil is another factor to consider when selecting the right soil for your balcony garden. Soils come in a variety of pH levels, ranging from acidic to alkaline. Plants have different pH requirements, so it is important to choose a soil with the appropriate pH level for your plants. A soil test can help you determine the pH level of the soil and can help you choose the right soil for your balcony garden.

4. Drainage: The drainage of the soil is an important factor to consider when selecting the right soil for your balcony garden. Poor drainage can lead to waterlogging and root rot, which can be detrimental to plant health. It is important to choose a soil that is well-draining, so that excess water can drain away and oxygen can reach the roots.

5. Organic Matter: The organic matter content of the soil is another important factor to consider when selecting the right soil for your balcony garden. Organic matter, such as compost and manure, improves the structure and nutrient content of the soil and can help to retain moisture and nutrients. It is important to choose a soil that contains a good amount of organic matter, so that it can provide adequate nutrition and moisture for your plants.

These are just a few of the important factors to consider when selecting the right soil for your balcony garden. It is important to choose a soil that is well-structured, nutrient-rich, has the right pH level, drains well, and contains a good amount of organic matter. Doing so will help ensure that your balcony garden is a success and that your plants will thrive.

Choosing the Right Plants for Your Balcony Garden

Gardening is an activity that has been around for centuries. It is a way to express creativity, bring life to an otherwise dull space, and even produce food. Balcony gardens are becoming increasingly popular as people are looking for ways to bring nature into their urban homes.

However, it can be difficult to know which plants are best suited for a balcony garden. This article will provide an overview of the different types of plants that can be used in a balcony garden, along with tips on choosing the right plants for your specific needs.

One of the most important things to consider when choosing plants for your balcony garden is the amount of sunlight the space receives. Different plants require different levels of sunlight to thrive, so it's important to know how much sun your balcony gets before you select plants.

Generally, balconies that face south, east, or west tend to receive the most sunlight, while balconies facing north will receive the least. When selecting plants, it's important to choose those that can handle the level of sunlight your balcony receives.

When selecting plants, it's also important to consider the size and shape of your balcony. If you have a small and narrow balcony, then you'll want to choose plants that are compact and won't take up too much space. You can find plants that are specifically designed for small spaces, such as trailing or vining plants. On the other hand, if you have a larger balcony, then you can choose plants that require more space, such as trees and shrubs.

In addition to the size and shape of your balcony, you should also consider the climate in which you live. Different plants have different requirements for temperature and humidity, so it's important to select plants that can tolerate the climate in your area. You can find a variety of plants that are suitable for your climate, so take some time to research before selecting plants.

Finally, when selecting plants for your balcony garden, it's important to think about the purpose of the garden. Do you want plants that will produce food, such as vegetables and herbs? Or do you want plants that will provide a sense of beauty and serenity? Knowing the purpose of your balcony garden can help you narrow down your options and select the right plants for your needs.

Choosing the right plants for your balcony garden can be a daunting task, but it doesn't have to be. By considering the amount of sunlight, size and shape of your balcony, climate, and purpose of the garden, you can select plants that are perfect for your space. With some research and careful consideration, you can create a beautiful and thriving balcony garden.

Preparing Your Balcony for Planting

Preparing your balcony for planting can be an exciting and rewarding experience. Not only will you be able to enjoy the beauty of your own little garden, but you will also be able to benefit from the health benefits of nature. Whether you are looking to create a lush green oasis or a small herb garden, there are a few tips to keep in mind when preparing your balcony for planting.

The first tip is to check with your building or landlord to ensure that you are allowed to plant on your balcony. Many buildings have restrictions on what sorts of plants or items can be placed on a balcony. It is also important to confirm that you are allowed to drill into the walls or balcony surface if necessary.

Once you have confirmed that you are able to plant on your balcony, it is important to assess the amount of sunlight that your balcony receives throughout the day. This will determine the types of plants that you can successfully grow on your balcony. For example, if your balcony receives a lot of direct sunlight, you should be able to grow vegetables, herbs and flowers with ease.

However, if your balcony is only exposed to indirect sunlight, you may need to choose plants that can thrive in partial shade.

The next step is to assess the condition of your balcony. If you have a wood deck, it is important to check for rot and splintering. If you find any signs of damage, it is important to repair them before you begin planting. Additionally, you should check for cracks in the grout between the tiles, as these can be a breeding ground for pests. If necessary, you should replace any damaged tiles or grout before planting.

The next step is to ensure that your balcony is properly sealed. This will help to protect your plants from the elements, as well as prevent water damage. You should also ensure that your balcony is equipped with a drainage system, as this will help to keep your plants healthy. If necessary, you should also purchase a waterproof mat to place beneath your plants to help protect them from the elements.

Finally, it is important to purchase the right soil and containers for your balcony planting. The soil should be specially formulated for container gardening, and you should also make sure that your containers are made from a material that is suitable for outdoor use. Additionally, you should make sure that your containers have adequate drainage holes, as this will help to keep your plants healthy.

Overall, preparing your balcony for planting can be a rewarding experience. By following these tips, you can ensure that your balcony garden is successful and that you are able to enjoy the beauty of nature in your own home.

Designing Your Balcony Garden

Designing a balcony garden is an exciting way to add a bit of nature to your living space. Whether you have a small outdoor space or a large balcony, you can create a beautiful garden oasis that will bring you joy and relaxation. With the right design and planning, you can have a garden that is both functional and aesthetically pleasing.

The first step in designing your balcony garden is to determine the size and shape of your balcony. If you have a large balcony, you can take advantage of the additional space to create a more elaborate design. If you have a smaller balcony, consider using vertical gardening to maximize your space. Once you've determined the size of your balcony, you can begin to plan out your design.

When it comes to designing a balcony garden, it's important to consider your climate and the amount of sunlight that your balcony receives. Depending on where you live, certain plants may not thrive in your climate. If you're in a sunny location, you can take advantage of this by planting sun-loving plants such as succulents, herbs, and other drought-tolerant plants. If you're in a colder climate, you may want to consider plants that can survive colder temperatures.

When planning your balcony garden, it's important to think about the types of plants that you'd like to grow. If you're looking for a low-maintenance garden, consider using plants that require minimal care such as succulents, cacti, and other drought-tolerant plants. If you're more of a green thumb, you can choose from a variety of flowers, vegetables, and herbs to create a colorful and vibrant garden.

Once you've decided on the types of plants that you'd like to grow, you can begin to think about the layout and design of your balcony garden. Consider adding a variety of containers, such as hanging baskets, window boxes, and planters, to help create a unique and interesting look. Consider using vertical gardening to save space and create a living wall of plants. If you have a larger balcony, you can create an outdoor living space by adding furniture, seating, and lighting.

When it comes to balcony garden design, there are endless possibilities. With a bit of planning and creativity, you can create a beautiful and inviting garden oasis that you can enjoy for years to come. Whether you're looking for a low-maintenance garden or a vibrant and colorful space, designing your balcony garden can be a fun and rewarding experience.

Selecting the Right Containers

When it comes to balcony gardening, selecting the right containers for your plants is essential for the success of your garden. A container garden is a great way to grow flowers, vegetables, and herbs, as well as other types of plants in a space-efficient and creative way. By choosing the right containers, you can create a beautiful, lush garden on your balcony that will provide you with years of enjoyment.

When selecting containers for your balcony garden, the most important factor to consider is size. Containers come in a wide variety of sizes, so it's important to choose ones that will fit the space you have available. The smaller the container, the more manageable it will be, but it will also limit the number of plants you can grow. You should also consider the weight of the container, as some may be too heavy to be hung or moved around.

In addition to size, you should also consider the material of the container.

Plastic containers are lightweight, easy to move, and relatively inexpensive. However, they can crack easily and may not be very durable in extreme weather conditions. Ceramic containers are more durable and can provide a more aesthetically pleasing look, but they can be more expensive and may be too heavy for your balcony. Wooden containers are a great choice for a natural look and are often more affordable, but they may need to be treated or painted to protect them from the elements.

When it comes to drainage, you should always make sure that your containers have adequate drainage holes. This will ensure that the soil and plants are not constantly soggy or drowning in water. If possible, select containers with a drainage tray to keep the excess water away from the roots of the plants.

Finally, the type of plants you are planning to grow should be taken into account when selecting containers. If you are growing vegetables or herbs, you should choose a container that allows enough room for the roots to spread. For flowers or ornamental plants, you will want to select a container that offers a visually pleasing design. If you need to move the containers around, consider opting for lightweight containers with handles.

Selecting the right containers for your balcony garden is essential for the success of your garden. By considering the size, material, drainage, and type of plants you are growing, you can choose the perfect containers for your balcony. With the right containers, you can create a beautiful and lush garden that you can enjoy for years to come.

Tools and Supplies for Balcony Gardening

Balcony gardening is becoming increasingly popular in urban areas due to the lack of available outdoor space. With the right tools and supplies, you can create a beautiful and productive balcony garden. From planters to irrigation systems, here is a list of essential tools and supplies for balcony gardening.

Planters: Planters are the foundation of any balcony garden. They will provide the right environment for your plants to grow and thrive. Make sure to choose the right size planter for your space and the type of plants you plan on growing. You can use plastic, ceramic, or metal planters depending on your personal preference.

Soil: High-quality soil is essential for any balcony garden. Make sure to get a soil that is specifically designed for container gardening. The soil should be light and airy to allow for adequate drainage. Compost is also a great way to add nutrients to your soil.

Irrigation System: A good irrigation system is essential for a successful balcony garden. You can use a hose, sprinkler system, or an automated drip irrigation system. Automated systems are the most efficient and require the least amount of maintenance.

Gardening Tools: Invest in a few basic gardening tools such as a trowel, rake, and shovel. These will come in handy when planting, weeding, and harvesting. You can also get a set of pruning shears for trimming and shaping plants.

Fertilizers: Fertilizers are essential for a healthy and productive balcony garden. Choose a fertilizer that is specifically designed for container gardening. Organic fertilizers are the best option as they are more nutrient-rich and have fewer chemicals.

Pesticides: Pesticides are important for keeping pests away from your balcony garden. Make sure to choose an organic pesticide that is safe for use on edible plants.

Lighting: If you plan on growing plants that need more light, you may need to invest in a few lighting fixtures. This can be anything from strings of lights to grow lights.

Ventilation: Proper ventilation is important for your balcony garden. You can use a fan or an exhaust fan to keep the air circulating.

Privacy Screen: If your balcony garden is visible from the street or from your neighbors, you may want to invest in a privacy screen. There are many different types of screens available, such as lattice panels, trellises, and bamboo screens.

These are just some of the essential tools and supplies for balcony gardening. With the right tools and supplies, you can create a beautiful and productive balcony garden.

What to Plant To Plant In Your Balcony Garden

Vegetables

Balcony gardens are a great way to grow vegetables in an urban environment. With a little bit of planning and preparation, you can create a thriving vegetable garden on your balcony. Consider the size of your balcony and the amount of sunlight it will receive. Some vegetables require at least 6 hours of direct sunlight everyday. If you have limited space, consider growing vegetables in containers or hanging planters. Plan out your garden design before planting. Place taller plants in the back and shorter plants in the front. You can also use trellises or stakes to help support your plants.

When it comes to planting, choose vegetables that are well-suited to the environment. Consider your local climate and the amount of sunlight and shade your balcony receives. Tomatoes, peppers, and greens are popular choices for balcony gardens. Many herbs and root vegetables, such as potatoes and carrots, are also good choices.

Be sure to use high quality soil, fertilizer, and compost. Container gardens require more frequent watering and fertilizing than in-ground gardens. Check the soil regularly and water when it is dry. Keep an eye out for pests and diseases, and take action if necessary.

With a bit of care and attention, you can create a beautiful and productive balcony garden. Planting vegetables on a balcony can provide you with fresh, nutritious produce all season long.

Fruits

Fruit trees can be a great addition to a balcony garden. Planting fruit trees on a balcony can provide a way to grow food and provide fresh, organic fruits in a limited space.

When planting fruit trees on a balcony, it is important to consider the size and weight of the tree and the space available. A balcony garden is usually limited in size, so it is important to select dwarf or semi-dwarf varieties of fruit trees that will stay small enough to fit in the available space. Additionally, it is important to consider the weight of the mature tree and the weight capacity of the balcony when selecting a variety.

Fruit trees will need to be planted in a container that is deep enough to provide the root system with room to spread out. It is important to have drainage holes on the container so as to allow easy flow of excess water to escape. The soil should be well-draining and nutrient rich, and a specialized potting mix can be used if needed.

Sunlight is also important when growing fruit trees on a balcony. Most varieties of fruit trees will need full sun, or at least 6 hours of direct sunlight each day. It is important to check the specific requirements of the variety of tree being planted and make sure it will get enough light on the balcony.

Fruit trees will also need regular watering and fertilizing to stay healthy and productive. It is important to check the soil moisture regularly and water when needed. Fertilizing should be done according to the specific needs of the tree and the soil type.

When planted and cared for properly, fruit trees can be a great addition to a balcony garden. Not only will they provide fresh, organic fruits, but they can also add beauty and interest to the space.

Herbs

Planting herbs on a balcony garden is a great way to bring a little bit of green into your home. Herbs are easy to maintain, aromatic, and can be used in a variety of recipes.

When planting herbs on a balcony garden, you'll need to consider the available space, light, and protection from wind. If you have limited space, you can opt for container gardening, which is great for growing a variety of herbs. You'll want to pick up containers that are at least six inches deep and have plenty of drainage holes.

For light, herbs need at least six hours of direct sunlight per day, so make sure to pick a spot on your balcony that gets enough sun. If your balcony is exposed to a lot of wind, you'll need to make sure your containers are securely anchored, or use wind screens or windbreaks to provide some protection.

When it comes to the soil, you'll want to use a soil mix that is specifically designed for herbs. This will ensure that your herbs get the necessary nutrients for healthy growth. Always ensure that the soil is well-drained.

Herbs are very versatile and can be used in a variety of recipes. Some great herbs to try growing on your balcony garden include basil, oregano, rosemary, thyme, chives, and mint.

Finally, make sure to water your herbs regularly and fertilize them once a month to ensure healthy growth. With some patience and care, you'll be able to enjoy your balcony herb garden in no time!

Flowers

Balcony gardening is an increasingly popular way to bring some of the outdoors inside. Planting flowers on your balcony can bring a sense of life and beauty to your home, while also creating an inviting and cozy atmosphere.

When planting flowers on your balcony, it's important to choose the right plants for your space. Consider the size of your balcony and the amount of sunlight it gets, as this will influence what types of plants you can choose. Some great options are petunias, marigolds, impatiens, and pansies. These flowers are bright and colorful, and they thrive in a variety of conditions.

When selecting containers for your flowers, be sure to choose ones that are appropriately sized for your plants. A pot that is too small will not provide your plants with enough room to grow.

Additionally, make sure to choose pots that have adequate drainage holes so that excess water can flow out freely.

Once you've chosen your plants and containers, it's important to prepare the soil. You can purchase potting soil from your local garden center or make your own soil mix from compost and peat moss. Make sure to mix the soil thoroughly and water the plants before planting.

When planting the flowers, start by digging a hole that is twice as wide as the potting container. Place the plant in the hole, and backfill with soil. Then tamp down the soil gently, and water evenly.

Once your plants are planted, it's important to care for them properly. Depending on the type of plants you have, you may need to water them daily or every other day. Additionally, you may need to remove any dead or wilted flowers regularly.

Planting flowers on your balcony can be a great way to add some life and beauty to your home. With a little bit of planning and preparation, you can create a stunning and inviting outdoor space.

Caring for Your Balcony Garden

Balcony gardens can be a wonderful way to enjoy nature in a small space. Caring for your balcony garden is essential to ensure it remains healthy, vibrant, and attractive. Here are some tips for taking care of your balcony garden.

Watering is a crucial part of caring for your balcony garden. Watering your plants regularly will keep them healthy and provide them with the nutrients they need. Make sure to check the soil moisture level to ensure that it is not too dry or too wet. Water in the morning so that the plants have the entire day to absorb the moisture.

Fertilizing is also important for your balcony garden. Use a balanced fertilizer that is specifically formulated for container plants. Apply the fertilizer every two to three weeks and follow the manufacturer's instructions.

Pruning is vital for keeping your balcony garden looking neat and tidy. Prune away any dead, dying, or diseased branches or leaves to keep your plants healthy. Pruning will also help to ensure that your plants have enough space to grow and spread.

Weeding is an important part of caring for your balcony garden. Pull out any weeds that are competing with your plants for nutrients and space. Be sure to wear gloves when weeding to avoid skin irritation.

Finally, it is important to provide your balcony garden with adequate sunlight. Sunlight helps to promote healthy growth and flowering. If your balcony does not get enough direct sunlight, you may need to supplement it with artificial lighting.

These tips will help you keep your balcony garden healthy and attractive. With the right care and attention, your balcony garden will be a source of joy and beauty for many years to come.

Watering and Maintenance for Your Balcony Garden

A balcony garden can provide a space to relax, entertain, and enjoy nature. But, like any garden, your balcony garden needs proper watering and maintenance to thrive. Without adequate water, your plants may suffer from heat and drought stress, causing them to become unhealthy and die. Learning how to properly water and maintain your balcony garden will ensure your plants stay healthy and vibrant for years to come.

Watering

The most important aspect of balcony garden maintenance is proper watering. Depending on the type of plants you have in your garden, the amount of water they need will vary. Some plants need more frequent watering, while others require less frequent watering.

Generally, plants should be watered once or twice a week, depending on the season and the type of plant. During hot, dry summer months, you may need to water your garden more often.

The best time of day to water your balcony garden is early in the morning. Watering in the morning allows the water to penetrate the soil and reach the roots of the plants before the sun gets too hot. It also minimizes water evaporation and maximizes the water absorption by the plants.

When watering your balcony garden, it’s important to use enough water so that the soil is moist, but not soggy. Overwatering can lead to root rot, which can kill your plants. To ensure your plants are getting enough water, use a soil moisture meter to measure the amount of water in the soil.

Maintenance

In addition to watering, your balcony garden also needs routine maintenance. To keep your garden healthy and attractive, you should remove any dead or dying plants, weeds, and debris. Pruning and trimming your plants will also help keep them looking their best.

You should also fertilize your balcony garden regularly. Fertilizer helps replenish the soil with essential nutrients, which helps ensure your plants stay healthy and vibrant. Depending on the type of fertilizer you use, you may need to apply it every few weeks or every month.

When you're done watering and maintaining your balcony garden, it's important to clean up any leftover debris. This will help discourage pests, diseases, and weeds.

Watering and maintaining your balcony garden is essential to keeping your plants healthy and vibrant. Proper watering and maintenance will ensure your plants stay healthy and attractive for years to come. With a little care and attention, your balcony garden can be a beautiful and relaxing oasis.

Conclusion

Balcony gardening can be a rewarding and enjoyable experience for any homeowner. Not only does it provide a space to relax and enjoy the outdoors, but it also provides an opportunity to bring a little bit of nature into the home. From plants and flowers to vegetables and fruits, balcony gardening can provide a variety of enjoyable experiences.

The first step in balcony gardening is to select the right location. Balconies should be sufficiently large enough to accommodate the desired plants, as well as provide adequate access to sunlight and water. When selecting plants and flowers, it is important to consider the climate and growing conditions in order to choose plants that will thrive in the environment.

Once the balcony is set up and the desired plants are chosen, it is important to maintain the garden. Plants need to be watered regularly and fertilized to keep them healthy. Pruning and trimming should be done on a regular basis to keep plants looking their best. Additionally, pests should be monitored and dealt with immediately in order to prevent any damage to plants.

One of the most enjoyable aspects of balcony gardening is the ability to watch plants grow and develop. Over time, plants will become more established and produce more flowers and fruit. This can be an incredibly satisfying experience, as gardeners watch their plants grow and flourish.

As with any type of gardening, balcony gardening can be a learning experience. Gardeners can experiment with different types of plants, flowers, and vegetables in order to determine which ones thrive in their environment. Additionally, balcony gardening can be a great way to teach children about the natural world and how plants grow.

Overall, balcony gardening can be an incredibly rewarding experience for any homeowner. From the satisfaction of watching plants grow to learn more about the natural world, balcony gardening can provide a variety of enjoyable experiences. Not only that, but it can also help to bring a little bit of nature into the home.

www.ingramcontent.com/pod-product-compliance
Lightning Source LLC
LaVergne TN
LVHW052101160826
845678LV00015B/3311

* 9 7 9 8 3 6 8 1 3 0 5 0 7 *